Government Contracting

Own Your Small Business

Julia Durand
Bridgeway 36 Consulting

1

Many learn that starting a business is the easy part, operating it is an entirely different process.

What I have learned after helping many just like you, despite your natural born talent or skill, is you must also have the mindset.

The first questions I will ask you may be found on page 7 of Start Your Business Today. Are you ready is the section.

Why do you want to start a business?

What do you do really well?

What is your passion area of expertise or skill?

MTV - My Time is Valuable and so is yours. Everything you need to know to start your business is provided in both books. I took the time to capture every step. I recently repeated the process and took out the first book "Start Your Business Today", I didn't need it, I knew it because I actually did the work myself.

Owning your own business requires a mindset that cannot be purchased without learning. Simply "buying" a book or "hiring" someone to do it for you only gets you in the game, you must preform to stay and create a steady stream of income to survive.

The purpose of this book is to introduce you to something every business needs to succeed, a revenue source. Every business needs customers, clients or consumers to generate revenue to operate the business and yes, pay yourself!

To Begin, You must have the following:

1. Business License

2. Sellers Permit(s)

If you do not have these items, please refer to my Starting a Business Guide www.bridgeway36.com or use your free consultation for a 15 min call.

Once you have your required Business License and Permit(s)

- A Duns Number is required for registration in the Government Contracting Data Base called SAM.

- The Duns Number is a registry of Business location. They collect data about your Business including location, credit worthiness and reputation Globally.

• You may obtain this free of charge at www.dnb.com

Small Businesses are the Economic Engine of this Country! You are well on your way to getting a piece of the American Pie.

1. Purchase a Bound Notebook and take notes each time you register for something. You will register for so many things you will not know how you got there or why. Having a paper trail allowed me to piece together this process. Often I landed somewhere and forgot my intended purpose as

there are many avenues to find your niche.

2. By far the most important step is your area of expertise, which categorized by **NAICS code.** Further detail will be provided however you need to complete the next step as there will be time in between registrations to research your "Niche". If you have completed the Goals Worksheet, you will be able to use that information to help you navigate that process.

3. Register yourself as an Entity in the Federal Database - SAM.gov

4. Write down your Registration information and passwords! Some have different password requirements and you will need a system for managing each.

- Registration confirmation can take up to 72 hours (Mine took 2 Hours pre Covid19).

- Once you are registered, you will need a CAGE Code. www.cage.dla.mil/home/usageAgree

- The Commercial and Government Entity **Code**, or **CAGE Code**, is a unique identifier assigned to; suppliers, various government or defense agencies, as well as government agencies themselves and various organizations. **CAGE** codes provide a standardized method of identifying a given facility at a specific location.

- The **NCAGE code** is a five-character alpha-numeric identifier assigned to entities located outside the United States by the NATO or NSPA organizations. When an entity is assigned a CAGE/**NCAGE,** the **code** is the same structure but it identifies which nation or if the NATO Support

Agency (NSPA), assigned the CAGE/**NCAGE**. (If you plan to export globally which can also be very profitable with many resources to assist you through the Small Business Administration).

- Read all the information provided during registration for the CAGE code, it is a blueprint to what you are able to do and what information will be asked of you during the Entity Registration.

  • You can pay an agency to do all of this for you. However, based on my experience, you will need to understand what you did **and** why, to fully understand what is available to you. Again, you must have the "Mindset" of an Owner and a desire to succeed, meaning it takes time and work.

- The Bound notebook will be a time saver as you will need to enter each of the License, Permits and Codes throughout your registration process. I suggest **reserving the second page of your notebook** just for these numbers and the corresponding password to each

website. The password re-
quirements vary so there is no
way to use one password for
each website.

- As you progress you will learn
that **there is a final step** that
will slow you down if you are
trying to accomplish this is a
short time frame (less than a
month, closer to two weeks).
To "time" the completion to
coincide with receipt of your
CAGE code, there is a mandatory Training required. **Use
this wait time to complete
the training for fast track
registration.**

- This step right here is the difference between success and succeeding.

"Success - the accomplishment of an aim or purpose"

"Succeeding - coming after something in time"

The difference is slight yet significant when you understand the mindset behind the difference. Often times we rest and wait while we congratulate ourselves on the accomplishment before us, however, the person who is driven to succeed will push as far as possible. How far can I go before I absolutely need the item. MTV - My Time is Valuable!

If you wait the posted two weeks to receive the required information only to find a mandatory training requirement is the next step? Depending upon your ability to process the material, it could take the full two weeks to take the course.

Please, give yourself time to process all the information presented.

- Read everything during the set-up process and take notes for things you don't understand as you will have to research it later, knowing when it was first asked of you will provide many clues to its purpose and importance. Remember, everything the Government requires of you is used to track something. If you go into it knowing this, you will be prepared to run your business with minimal assistance.

- Registration as a Small Business is included in the questions asked during the CAGE registration stage. This is important as the process to certify is self-certification until June

2020. At that point you will have to go through a Third Party Vendor. You will also want to register with the SBA once you receive the approval for your CAGE Code. Make sure to link your _____ registration with your SBA.CERTIFY registration.

The Federal Contracting Business is a similar to a huge Jigsaw Puzzle and it touches every aspect of our lives. The opportunities awaiting you through Government Contracts can be lucrative and vast.

This arti- cle was post- ed February 1, 2021 fol- lowing President Joe Biden's un- veiling of his Made In America iniative that mirrored his Build Back Better proposal used during the 2020 election.

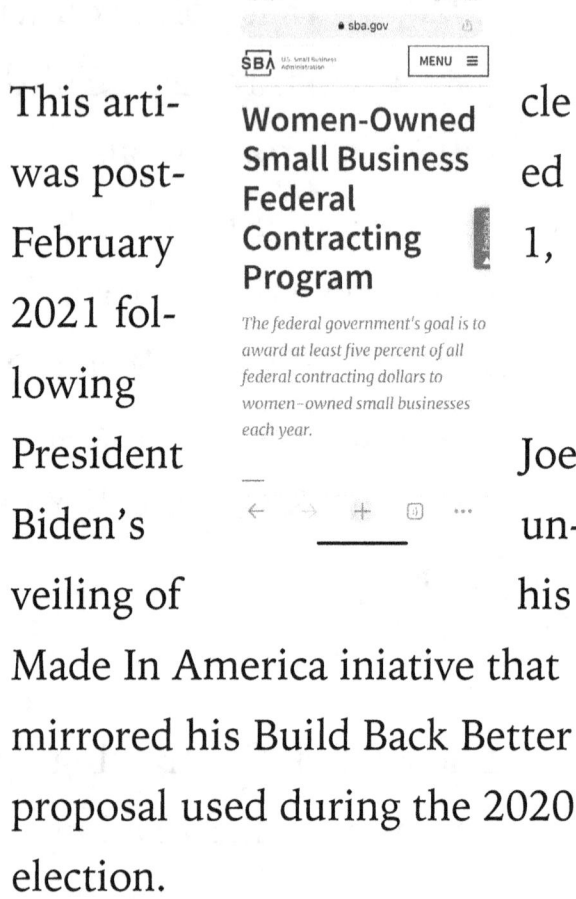

Five Percent of all contracting dollars will be awarded
to Small Women Owned
Business.

You may become over-
whelmed and veer off into
different directions once you

understand the various layers of government contracting opportunities.

This is expected and why you should stop before you go too far. It's okay to venture! I did, however, until you learn the Government Databases, I would leave bread crumbs so that you can return to your last location. It's okay as long as you remember to document where you left off or where you went to, find your system so that you can return to where you started. I call it, letting the system lead you as opposed to you directing your own path.

- You will find the list of NAIC codes here https://www.naics.com/search/. You will want to research this list thoroughly as there are sub categories which agencies use to pin point the exact contract search. You may want to include several to make sure you are included in the search for your true service or product.

Please identify these codes and write them down with the title while you wait for your CAGE number to arrive.

- These codes are required for the steps below; (Entity Registration and Representations). This is where you agree to the legal terms of contracting and you assign Authorized Point of Contact (POC) and signers of your Government Contracts.

- You will have to have your telephone number and website at some point. I had an existing website however I did not provide the web address as it was geared toward a separate business and I did not want to connect the two until it is redesigned to host a government friendly image. They will check.

- Once I decided on my "government" business I had to start the process over, however, I did learn that the CAGE and DUNS number are associated with your name. All that was required was an update of the Entity information.

- Complete the Required Training Now

- Vendor Support Center -

- https://www.gsa.gov/small-business/-become-a-gsa-vendor/register-your-business. This is where you will find the required training to do business with the Federal Government. There is also a list that identifies each of the aforementioned steps. While you could start here, you would miss the importance of the registration process and understanding of the "Total" process. You must do this on your own even though there are agencies that will walk you through it for a fee. Use it if you need to or do not have the time and have an understanding of the process. The education received is valuable.

- Begin taking this online training while you wait for your cage code and small business/ disadvantaged business classification.

  • During this training, take lots of notes. I was familiar with the procurement process and many of the terms, however, some I forgot. Create a glossary of terms to be familiar with like FOB - Free on Board. it means once you the supplier ship your product, the Buyer (Federal Government) accepts delivery of goods. Its no longer in your hands or responsibility.

• Terms will appear repeatedly, it is important that you have a full understanding of these terms when reading Contract Bids. Remember, you are the sole point of responsibility. It is YOUR responsibility to know what YOU are doing at all times. The BUCK Starts and Stops with YOU.

• Small Business Size Standards requires understanding when bidding on contracts. A contract could remove you from your small business classification.

- Once you complete the training all you have to do is wait for your CAGE number and narrow down your NAICS codes.

• I took copious notes during the training. It answered so many questions and provided additional terms to be familiar with for contracting opportunities as well as resources to further accelerate your ability to bid on government contracts.

- You will want to capture the various "other" sites the training directs you too, however, practice restraint and focus on completing the training as opposed to following rabbit holes. It's all great information trust me, and it's what you want and need to know, however, getting all of it and completing the course makes it all applicable once you know how to navigate the process.

- You will want to create a profile at GSA.gov as you will return frequently. Look for eLibrary gsaelibrary - CCR (Contract Registry), GSA Advantage, CTA Contractor Team Arrangement.

- You will learn about funding vehicles and terms like Blanket Purchase Agreement (BPA). Once you receive your CAGE code, you will want to review the notice and become familiar with the information they provide. I would print it to review at a later time when you become over-whelmed with possibilities and need to focus on how you initially registered

- Login to your SAM.Gov Account to Register your Business as an Entity Remember this cannot be completed until you receive your CAGE code.

- At SAM.GOV you will be allowed to enter your business data. Have the following:

- Taxpayer Information - Remember those Business License and Permits I mentioned FIRST... They are required now including your Business Bank Account.

- A Business Bank Account is required to keep separate receipts. If you ever request a SBA (Small Business Association) Loan, they will want to see that you have a way to identify and separate your actual business expenses.

- POS System - Point of Sale - Square, Paypal etc. (Card Readers)

- If you use an existing personal account as I did, make sure you write it down! The Government will automatically send your payments electronically to the bank account you enter at this point. It must be used for that business entity only. At some point you will want to take advantage of a Business Banking Account. Your EIN number is required to open this account. Separate banking requirements exist for International sales.

- Entity - Registration and Representations is where you

will tell the Federal Government about your service or product by way of a NAICS code: The North American Industry Classification System (**NAICS**) is the standard used by Federal statistical agencies in classifying business establishments for the purpose of collecting, analyzing, and publishing statistical data related to the U.S. business economy. Don't worry about finding the "exact" match for your codes as you may change them at any time, and you will as you progress through this process you will have access to information that will gear you towards a code that matches contract language specific to "small business entities". This is covered in the How to Respond to an RFP Course.

It was at this point in the process that I came into contact with a Small Business offering workshops that introduced small businesses to Procurement officers from all branches of Government. I suggest you use the resources provided in the Vendor Training to locate such workshops in your area. They are your ticket to contacts.

At some point you will have to submit an RFP, Grant or some other method to identify the Services or Products being contracted. Bridgeway36 is available to assist you through that process as well.

Here's to your success and please contact us with any questions, or to schedule an individual consultation. www.Bridgeway36.com

You can be an economic engine for the economy!

_____

_____

_____

_____